Harold R Foster

Prince Valiant

COMPRISING PAGES 1948 THROUGH 1991

Karak the Terrible

FANTAGRAPHICS BOOKS

ABOUT THIS EDITION:

Produced in cooperation with the Danish publisher Carlsen and several other publishers around the world, this new edition of PRINCE VALIANT is intended to be the definitive compilation of Hal Foster's masterpiece.

In addition to this volume, Fantagraphics Books has in stock 31 more collections of Foster's Valiant work (Vols. 2, 9-33, 39-43). After completing the 40-volume run of Foster's series, we are now continuing with the John Cullen Murphy drawn continuation of the strip.

ABOUT THE PUBLISHER:

FANTAGRAPHICS BOOKS has dedicated itself to bringing readers the finest in comic book and comic strip material, both new and old. Its "classics" division includes *The Complete E.C. Segar Popeye*, the *Complete Little Nemo in Slumberland* hardcover collection, and *Pogo* and *Little Orphan Annie* reprints. Its "modern" division is responsible for such works as *Love and Rockets* by Los Bros. Hernandez, Peter Bagge's *Hate*, Daniel Clowes's *Eightball*, Chris Ware's *ACME*, and American editions of work by Muñoz & Sampayo, Lewis Trondheim, and F. Solano Lopez, as well as *The Complete Crumb Comics*.

PREVIOUS VOLUMES IN THIS SERIES:

PRINCE VA;LIANT, Volume 44
"Karak the Terrible"
comprising pages 1948 (June 9, 1974) through 1991 (April 6, 1975)
Published by Fantagraphics Books, 7563 Lake City Way NE, Seattle, WA 98115
Editorial Co-Ordinator: Henning Kure and Jens Trasborg
Cover colored by Jesper Ejsing
Cover inked by Jan Kjær Jensen
Fantagraphics Books staff: Kim Thompson and Peppy White
Copyright © 2001 King Features Syndicate, Inc., Bull's, Interpresse, & Fantagraphics Books, Inc.
Printed in Denmark   ISBN 1-56097-469-9   First Printing: Winter, 2001/2002

Prince Valiant
IN THE DAYS OF KING ARTHUR
BY HAL FOSTER

Our Story: ONCE MORE GAWAIN AND ARN ARE HOMEWARD BOUND, BUT GAWAIN GRUMBLES: "YOUR GALLANTRY IS EXCEEDED ONLY BY YOUR STUPIDITY. NOW WE ARE SADDLED WITH A WOMAN, SERVANTS AND BAGGAGE. WE WILL NEVER GET TO PARIS!"

BUT LADY MELLICENT KNOWS THE SHORTEST WAY, THE BEST ROADS AND EACH EVENING BRINGS THEM TO SOME WELCOME VILLA OR CASTLE.

FINALLY THEY CROSS THE BRIDGE TO THE ISLAND OF THE CITY OF PARIS. THERE IS GREAT EXCITEMENT, FOR THE KING HAS CHOSEN THIS AS HIS NEW CAPITAL.

JEAN DE BERRY HAS SPENT A PLEASANT WINTER AT COURT WHERE HE HAS BEEN QUITE A FAVORITE WITH THE LADIES. HE IS ENGROSSED WITH HIS MOST RECENT CONQUEST, WHEN HE HEARS VOICES RAISED IN GREETING: "WELCOME TO PARIS, SIR GAWAIN!"

IMPATIENT AT THIS INTERRUPTION TO HIS GLIB LOVEMAKING, HE GLANCES DOWN. THERE STANDS THE HANDSOME KNIGHT, A RED-HEADED YOUTH OF NOBLE BEARING AND BETWEEN THEM, HER FACE ALIGHT WITH PLEASURE, THE LADY MELLICENT, HIS WIFE!

SHE SHOULD NOT BE HERE WITHOUT HIS PERMISSION, BUT HE CANNOT GET THROUGH THE THRONG TO SCOLD HER. HOW EMBARRASSING IT IS TO SEE HIS MEEK LITTLE WIFE THE CENTER OF ATTENTION WHILE HE IS LEFT OUT.

AT LAST HE FINDS HER ALONE. "WHY DID YOU COME HERE WITHOUT MY CONSENT?" HE DEMANDS. "TO BE WITH YOU. AREN'T YOU GLAD?" SHE LAUGHS, "COME LET US DANCE."

NEVER BEFORE HAD SHE ACTED WITHOUT HIS CONSENT. IS HE LOSING HIS AUTHORITY? SHE HAS CHANGED, LOOKS YOUNGER, HAPPIER. BUT HE MUST CHANGE ALL THAT AND ONCE AGAIN BE MASTER.

NEXT WEEK— Tamed

1948   6-9

Prince Valiant
IN THE DAYS OF KING ARTHUR
BY HAL FOSTER

Our Story: JEAN DE BERRY HAD BEEN A COURT FAVORITE, ESPECIALLY WITH THE LADIES, AND THE ARRIVAL OF HIS MEEK LITTLE WIFE IS EMBARRASSING. AS HIS ANGER WAXES, HIS CHARM WANES.

HE CANNOT REPRIMAND HER. HE CANNOT EVEN GET NEAR HER, FOR SHE IS CONSTANTLY SURROUNDED BY A MERRY THRONG. WHAT IS THE ATTRACTION? IS IT THE HANDSOME SIR GAWAIN AND THE YOUNG PRINCE.....?

....OR COULD IT BE THE LADY MELLICENT? NOT SINCE THEIR HONEYMOON HAVE HER EYES SPARKLED THUS, HER FACE SO AGLOW. SHE LOOKS ALMOST PRETTY, NAY, BEAUTIFUL!

OH, HOW UNCONVENTIONAL! HE FALLS IN LOVE WITH HIS OWN WIFE! PRECEDED BY A BOX OF BONBONS AND A HUGE BOUQUET OF FLOWERS, HE GOES TO MELLICENT'S ROOM. AND WHAT HAPPENS THERE, THOUGH IMPORTANT TO THEM, IS NO CONCERN OF OURS....

...SUFFICIENT TO STATE THAT THEY BEGIN A SENTIMENTAL JOURNEY BACK HOME, MELLICENT RIDING PILLION WITH HER ARMS AROUND HER HUSBAND WHILE HE WEARS THAT SILLY GRIN THAT MARKS A LOVER. SIR GAWAIN DESCRIBES THE INCIDENT THUS:

"MUSH! ARN, YOU ARE AS SILLY AS YOUR FATHER, ALWAYS CONTRIVING THOSE 'HAPPY ENDINGS' LIKE HONEY INSIDE ONE'S ARMOR. BAH!"

SPRING ARRIVES AND THE WINTER STORMS ABATE. SIR GAWAIN FINDS A SHIP THAT WILL TAKE HIM TO BRITAIN.

BUT ARN MUST RIDE TO THE COAST WHERE VIKING SHIPS OFTEN SPEND THE WINTER AWAITING CALMER WEATHER FOR THEIR JOURNEY BACK TO THULE.

NEXT WEEK – The Meadhall   6-16

1949

Prince Valiant
IN THE DAYS OF KING ARTHUR
BY HAL FOSTER

Our Story: PRINCE ARN RIDES THE WINDY COAST SEEKING A SHIP TO TAKE HIM TO THULE. HOW LONELY IT IS WITHOUT SIR GAWAIN. FOR THE TIME OF PARTING HAD COME AND HIS MERRY COMPANION IS ON HIS WAY TO BRITAIN.

IN A SHELTERED COVE HE FINDS A PARTY OF VIKINGS. THEY HAVE WINTERED HERE, BUT NOW THAT SPRING HAS ARRIVED THE SHIPS ARE READIED FOR THE HOMEWARD JOURNEY.

PRINCE ARN IS WELCOMED. NOT ONLY IS IT AN HONOR TO SAIL WITH THE GRANDSON OF THEIR KING, BUT HE ALSO HAS GOLD TO PAY FOR HIS PASSAGE.

IN THEIR SMOKY MEAD HALL, LIT BY THE LURID GLARE OF PINE KNOT TORCHES, THEY HOLD HIGH WASSAIL IN HONOR OF THEIR PRINCE. MANY A TOAST IS OFFERED AND ARN MUST RESPOND TO EACH, AND THE MEAD IS STRONG. THEY HAVE REASON TO CELEBRATE, FOR IT HAS BEEN A COLD AND STORMY WINTER AND ON THE MORROW THEY SAIL FOR HOME.

NEXT WEEK—Heroics

6-23

1950

Our Story: ON THE MORROW THEY BEGIN THEIR HOMEWARD JOURNEY, SO TODAY THEY CELEBRATE THEIR RELEASE FROM THE BOREDOM OF WINTER QUARTERS. THE SMOKY MEAD HALL ECHOES WITH JOYOUS SHOUTS AS CUPS ARE FILLED AGAIN AND AGAIN.

COURTESY DEMANDS THAT ARN ACKNOWLEDGE EACH TOAST, TOO MANY IN FACT, AND HE BECOMES SLEEPY.

NOW THE MOOD CHANGES. THEY BEGIN TO BOAST OF THEIR PROWESS, HOLDING ALOFT THEIR WEAPONS AND TELLING OF HEROIC DEEDS. SOON THEY HAVE WORKED THEMSELVES INTO A FRENZY, THE BATTLE LUST IS UPON THEM.

THEN JARNSAXA, THEIR CAPTAIN, ARISES: "LET US NOW PROVE WE MAKE NO IDLE BOASTS! OLAF REGAN AND HIS MEN ARE WINTERING THREE LEAGUES TO THE EAST. WE WILL MARCH AGAINST THEM AND PROVE OUR MIGHT, SHIELD TO SHIELD!"

ARN IS READY TO GO..... NOT ON THE RAID, BUT TO BED. HOWEVER HE IS SWEPT ALONG WITH THE BERSERKERS.

6-30　　　　　　　　1951

THE DAY IS ALMOST SPENT AS THEY SET OUT ON THEIR FORAY, AND THE CASK OF MEAD IS TAKEN ALONG IN CASE THEIR SPIRITS LAG ON THE ROUGH JOURNEY ALONG THE ROCKY COAST.

NEXT WEEK - The March to Nowhere

Prince Valiant
IN THE DAYS OF KING ARTHUR
BY HAL FOSTER

Our Story: INSPIRED BY THEIR OWN BOASTING AND INFLAMED WITH MEAD, JARNSAXA AND HIS CREW MARCH ON THE WINTER CAMP OF OLAF REGAN TO PROVE THEIR HARDIHOOD IN BATTLE.

IT IS A ROUGH ROAD TO TRAVEL AND THEY STOP OFTEN TO RENEW THEIR FIGHTING SPIRIT FROM A CASK BROUGHT ALONG FOR MEDICINAL PURPOSES.

IT IS DAWN WHEN THEY REACH THEIR GOAL AND HALT IN DISMAY......

....OLAF REGAN HAS PUT TO SEA ON HIS HOMEWARD VOYAGE, LEAVING ONLY THE MESS OF THEIR WINTERING. "WE WILL BURN THEIR MEAD HALL!" SHOUTS JARNSAXA, "PERHAPS THEY WILL RETURN AND OFFER US BATTLE!"

"SIT DOWN," A SLEEPY VOICE GROWLS, "IF THEY SEE US HERE THEY WILL KNOW OUR CAMP IS UNGUARDED, AND THEY CAN REACH IT BY SEA AND PLUNDER IT BEFORE WE CAN GET THERE BY LAND."

GONE NOW IS THE WARLIKE SPIRIT, AND THE MEAD THAT MADE EACH MAN FEEL LIKE A HERO HAS BEEN CONSUMED.

THE EMPTY CASK IS THROWN ASIDE AND YOUNG ARN IS PUT IN ITS PLACE. BUT ALL IS NOT LOST, FOR THIS FIASCO HAS CONTRIBUTED TO HIS EDUCATION AND IT WILL BE A LONG TIME BEFORE HE EVER AGAIN SEES THE BOTTOM OF A MEAD CUP.

NEXT WEEK - *The Doubtful Haven*

1952

7-7

Prince Valiant
IN THE DAYS OF KING ARTHUR
BY HAL FOSTER

Our Story: THE SHIP IS LAUNCHED FOR THE HOMEWARD JOURNEY. THIS SHOULD BE A JOYOUS OCCASION, BUT THE VIKINGS HAVE CELEBRATED THEIR RELEASE FROM WINTER CAMP AND THEY EXIT QUARRELING.

SAILING UP THE CHANNEL IN FINE WEATHER, ARN HAS TIME FOR DREAMING OF LYDIA. HAS SHE FORGOTTEN HIM, OR FOUND ANOTHER? NEVER HAS HER FACE BEEN SO CLEAR IN HIS DREAMS.

AS THEY PASS DOVER, THE NORTH SEA GREETS THEM WITH A GREAT STORM. THEY CANNOT LAND, FOR WITH A LEE SHORE, THEIR SHIP WOULD BE DASHED TO PIECES IN THE SURF.

NIGHT AND DAY THE STRUGGLE GOES ON UNTIL, NEAR EXHAUSTION, THEY FIND SHELTER IN THANET. BUT STILL THEY HAVE NO REST, FOR THE SEAMS IN THE HULL HAVE OPENED.

ON A NEARBY BEACH THEIR TREASURE IS UNLOADED AND THE SHIP DRAWN UP TO BE CAULKED AND TARRED, AND ARN IS FREE TO WANDER ABOUT THE TOWN. CURIOSITY LEADS HIM TO THE ANCIENT ROMAN CASTLE WHICH KING ARTHUR HAD REPAIRED AND GARRISONED.

THE OFFICER AT THE GATE, A TALL, HANDSOME KNIGHT, GREETS ARN COURTEOUSLY AND UPON LEARNING HIS RANK INTRODUCES HIM TO LORD GILFORD, THE GOVERNOR.

AND THE GOVERNOR IS NOT PLEASED. HE HAS HAD SOME UNFORTUNATE DEALINGS WITH VIKINGS AND IS ANNOYED THAT COURTESY DEMANDS HE ENTERTAIN THE GRANDSON OF A VIKING KING.

AS ARN LEAVES THE CHAMBER, A SMILING YOUTH HAILS HIM: "PAY NO ATTENTION TO MY FATHER'S GROWLING. HE BELIEVES ALL VIKINGS ARE BAD. LET US GO FIND SOME ENTERTAINMENT."

1953   NEXT WEEK – The Rivals 7-14

Prince Valiant

Prince **Valiant** IN THE DAYS OF KING ARTHUR BY HAL FOSTER

Our Story: AFTER THE CHILLY RECEPTION OF LORD GILFORD, THE GOVERNOR, THE CHEERFUL GREETING OF HIS SON, HECTOR, IS A PLEASING CONTRAST.

AT THE FORTRESS GATES, HECTOR INTRODUCES ARN TO THE LOVELY LADY MAUD AS 'MY FUTURE WIFE.' SHE ACKNOWLEDGES THE INTRODUCTION WITH UNSMILING COURTESY.......

......THEN TURNS AND WALKS TO THE GATEWAY AND STANDS BESIDE TALL ARNOLD, A GESTURE THAT TELLS ALL TOO PLAINLY WHOM SHE PREFERS.

"POOR MAUD," GRINS HECTOR, "I DON'T BELIEVE SHE LOVES SIR ARNOLD. WE WERE ONLY CHILDREN WHEN THE MARRIAGE CONTRACT WAS SIGNED SO THAT TWO POWERFUL FAMILIES WOULD BE UNITED THROUGH OUR MARRIAGE. SHE WANTS ROMANCE, NOT POLITICS."

THEY ARE SEATED IN A TAVERN WHEN SIR ARNOLD ENTERS AND IS INVITED TO JOIN THEM. ARN ADMIRES THIS QUIET KNIGHT, TALL AND STRONG, A CONTRAST TO HIS SLENDER RIVAL.

IT IS A PLEASANT CONVERSATION, FOR EACH HAS MANY INTERESTING ADVENTURES TO RELATE, BUT THROUGH IT ALL ARN SENSES THE BITTER ENMITY BETWEEN THE RIVALS.

AS THEY LEAVE THE TAVERN HECTOR SAYS, "THANET IS A ROUGH TOWN, SO GO ARMED. EVEN I WEAR A MAILED SHIRT BENEATH MY FRIPPERIES!"

1454   7-21

LADY MAUD GOES SHOPPING IN THE MARKETPLACE ACCOMPANIED BY TWO GUARDS AND A SERVANT TO CARRY HER PURCHASES. HER DELICATE BEAUTY, A SHARP CONTRAST TO THE ROWDY POPULACE.

NEXT WEEK—The Price of Violence

Prince Valiant

IN THE DAYS OF KING ARTHUR

BY HAL FOSTER

OUR STORY: THEY MEET LADY MAUD AND HER GUARDS IN THE MARKETPLACE AND OFFER THEIR ADDED PROTECTION, FOR THIS IS A ROUGH DISTRICT.

SIR ARNOLD IS VERY POSSESSIVE AS HE SHOULDERS ARN AND HECTOR ASIDE AND TAKES THE LADY'S ARM.

IT IS A SMALL INCIDENT: A TIPSY YOKEL TRIPS, MUTTERING A SWEARWORD, AND JOSTLES THE LADY.

IT MIGHT HAVE GONE UNNOTICED AS JUST A CLUMSY ACCIDENT, BUT ARNOLD STRIKES THE DRUNKEN FELLOW A VICIOUS BLOW ON THE EYE.

THE UNRULY CROWD HAS NO LOVE FOR THE PEACEKEEPERS FROM THE CASTLE, AND THIS ACT OF BRUTALITY BRINGS A HOWL OF ANGER. A STONE IS HURLED, THEN ANOTHER... KNIVES ARE DRAWN......

...."RUN!" YELLS ARNOLD, AND GRASPING MAUD BY THE ARM SPRINTS FOR THE SAFETY OF THE GATES — LEAVING ARN, HECTOR AND THE TWO GUARDS TO HOLD BACK THE ENRAGED MOB.

1955

7-28

SO IT IS TALL ARNOLD WHO BRINGS THE LADY MAUD ACROSS THE DRAW-BRIDGE TO THE SAFETY OF THE CASTLE NEXT WEEK—*Up the Drawbridge!*

Prince Valiant
IN THE DAYS OF KING ARTHUR
by HAL FOSTER

Our Story: IT IS TALL SIR ARNOLD WHO, WITH DRAWN SWORD, RACES THROUGH THE BARBICAN GATE, ACROSS THE DRAWBRIDGE AND BRINGS THE LADY MAUD TO THE SAFETY OF THE CASTLE. LEAVING ARN, HECTOR AND THE TWO ARMED GUARDS TO HOLD OFF THE ANGRY MOB.

"*UP THE DRAWBRIDGE!*" COMMANDS ARNOLD. "*WHAT! LEAVE YOUR FRIENDS AT THE MERCY OF THE MOB?*" CRIES MAUD. "*IT IS MY DUTY TO PROTECT THE CASTLE,*" ANSWERS ARNOLD.

"*FALSE KNIGHT! COWARD!*" SCREAMS MAUD, AND RUNS INTO THE COURTYARD.
"*HO, THE GUARD! TO ARMS!*" SHE CRIES. WARNED BY THE NOISE OF THE RIOT, THE SOLDIERS ARE READY AND RESPOND TO HER CRY.

MEANWHILE, MAKING A STAND IN THE GATEWAY, HECTOR, WHO IS WITHOUT A HELMET, GOES DOWN...STRUCK BY A HURLED STONE. IT LOOKS AS IF ARNOLD HAS LOST A RIVAL.

NOW, WITH HIS TROOP LINED UP BEHIND HIM, SIR ARNOLD ORDERS THE DRAW-BRIDGE LOWERED AND MARCHES OUT AT THEIR HEAD.

FIRST TO REACH HECTOR IS THE LADY MAUD. SHE HAD HATED HIM ONLY BECAUSE SHE WAS BEING FORCED INTO A MARRIAGE OF CONVENIENCE. HOW BRAVELY HE HAS FOUGHT FOR HER SAFETY!

AT SUNSET SIR ARNOLD RETURNS AT THE HEAD OF HIS VETERAN SOLDIERS. THERE IS BLOOD ON THEIR SWORDS, BEHIND THEM, SMOKE AND FLAMES. ARNOLD HAS DONE HIS DUTY.
1956   NEXT WEEK— *Noble to the Last*   8-4

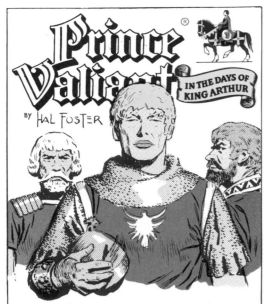

Prince Valiant IN THE DAYS OF KING ARTHUR

BY HAL FOSTER

Our Story: SIR ARNOLD RETURNS, PROUD THAT HE HAS TAUGHT THE UNRULY TOWNSPEOPLE A LESSON. HE IS RECEIVED IN SILENCE, BUT HE DOES NOT CARE. HE HAS DONE HIS DUTY.

IN THE CROWDED FORTRESS, HECTOR RECEIVES THE TENDEREST OF CARE WHILE ARN, WHO FOUGHT WITHOUT A SHIELD, HAS A BROKEN ARM SET.

LORD GILFORD, RETURNING FROM A VISIT TO HIS FIEF, SEES THE SMOKE RISING FROM THE TOWN AND FEARS A VIKING RAID OR THE RETURN OF THE SAXONS.

ON LEARNING THE TRUTH, HE SUMMONS ARNOLD: "WHY DID YOU BURN HALF THE TOWN AND SLAUGHTER HALF THE CITIZENS, AND WHY DID YOU LEAVE MY SON HECTOR TO THE ANGRY MOB?" "IT IS MY DUTY TO PROTECT THE CASTLE, MY LORD." THE GOVERNOR'S EYES BLAZE: "GET OUT!" HE WHISPERS.

"FAREWELL, SIR ARN. I RIDE TO CAMELOT TO BECOME A KNIGHT OF THE ROUND TABLE AND SERVE KING ARTHUR." THE PAIN OF HIS BROKEN ARM MAKES ARN SHORT TEMPERED: "KING ARTHUR HAS BETTER MEN THAN YOU IN HIS STABLE," HE SNAPS.

A DAY OF VIOLENCE COMES TO ITS TRAGIC CLOSE, AND TWO YOUNG LOVERS ARE RECONCILED. THE PRICE OF ROMANCE SEEMS EXCESSIVE.

SIR ARNOLD MOUNTS HIS WAR-HORSE AND RIDES TOWARD CAMELOT, NOBLE TO THE LAST.

1957 © King Features Syndicate, Inc., 1974. World rights reserved.

ARN IS IN DESPAIR, AS HIS JOURNEY HOMEWARD SUFFERS ONE DELAY AFTER ANOTHER. WILL LYDIA STILL WAIT FOR HIS RETURN? DOES SHE REMEMBER?

NEXT WEEK—*The Coast of Thule*

Our Story: SPRING GLIDES INTO SUMMER AND ARN IS IN DESPAIR. THE COUNTLESS DELAYS TO HIS HOMEWARD JOURNEY, THE UNCERTAINTY OF HIS RECEPTION THERE, AND THE PAIN OF HIS BROKEN ARM ADD TO HIS MISERY.

HE LEAVES THE GRIM FORTRESS TO STAY WITH HIS CREW AND SPEED THE REPAIRS TO THE SHIP. AT LAST IT IS SEAWORTHY AND IS LAUNCHED FOR THE LONG JOURNEY NORTH.

AT LAST! THE COAST OF THULE RISES IN ALL ITS AWESOME GRANDEUR. THE SKALD TAKES UP HIS HARP AND THE OARSMEN SING AS THEY ROW. ARN REMOVES THE SPLINTS AND PAINFULLY, BUT CHEERFULLY, BEGINS TO EXERCISE HIS ARM.

NEXT WEEK– *Midsummer's Eve*   8-18

Prince Valiant
IN THE DAYS OF KING ARTHUR
BY HAL FOSTER

Our Story: THE LONG JOURNEY NEARS ITS END. VIKINGSHOLM IS IN SIGHT. THEN ARN SEES THE GAILY DECORATED BOATS THAT CROWD THE BEACH. HE COUNTS THE NOTCHES ON THE CALENDAR-STICK.... IT IS MIDSUMMER'S EVE!

HE MAKES HIS WAY THROUGH THE MERRYMAKERS, EAGER TO SEE HIS MOTHER, AND THEN SEARCH FOR LYDIA.

ALETA SEES HIM COMING AND HER LONG VIGIL IS ENDED. HE HAD SAILED AWAY A BROKENHEARTED BOY AND HAS RETURNED A STALWART YOUTH. SOON SHE WILL HOLD HER SON IN LOVING EMBRACE.

SHE WATCHES HIS COMING. HE REACHES THE STEPS...... THEN HESITATES, SEARCHING THE DANCERS FOR ONE SPECIAL FACE, AND SLOWLY DESCENDS.
ALETA SMILES AWAY HER TEARS, FOR SHE KNOWS THE TIME HAS COME WHEN A MOTHER MUST SHARE HER SON WITH SOME GIRL.

HE FINDS LYDIA IN THE SAME GLADE WHERE SHE HAD KISSED HIM AND SAID GOOD-BYE. BOTH HAVE CHANGED DURING THEIR LONG SEPARATION, BUT THE LIGHT IN THEIR EYES SHOWS THE CHANGE IS FOR THE BETTER.

THE MUSIC AND LAUGHTER COME FAINTLY THROUGH THE GLADE AND THE HOURS PASS.

ARN LEAPS TO HIS FEET. "COME, WE MUST GO FIND MOTHER."
"YOU GO, I WILL FOLLOW LATER," AND SHE GIVES HIM A PUSH, "THAT MOMENT IS FOR YOUR MOTHER ALONE."

SO QUEEN ALETA GREETS HER SON AND ALL THE ANXIOUS DAYS OF WAITING ARE FORGOTTEN. SHE IS CONTENT.

8-2 NEXT WEEK - A Call for Help

1959

Prince Valiant
IN THE DAYS OF KING ARTHUR
BY HAL FOSTER

Our Story: PRINCE ARN RETURNS FROM HIS LONG ABSENCE AND THE ROYAL FAMILY OF THULE ARE ALL TOGETHER ONCE MORE. ARN TELLS OF HIS ADVENTURES, AND VAL APPROVES HIS SON'S SELF-RELIANCE. ALETA WORRIES ABOUT HIS RECKLESSNESS, WHILE GALAN SO ADMIRES HIS BROTHER.....

.....THAT HE, TOO, SALLIES FORTH IN SEARCH OF ADVENTURE, GETS LOST AND HAS TO BE TRACKED DOWN WITH THE HOUNDS.

ARN AND LYDIA HAVE TO MAKE UP FOR THEIR LONG SEPARATION AND SPEND ENTIRE DAYS TOGETHER. THEY BOTHER NO ONE.

NOT SO THE TWINS.... THEY TRY TO TURN ARN'S HOME-COMING INTO A LONG MISCHIEVOUS HOLIDAY, BUT ARE SENT BACK TO THEIR STUDIES.

IT IS A TIME OF PEACE AND PLENTY IN THE KINGDOM OF THULE, SO THE KING AND PRINCE VALIANT GO HUNTING TOGETHER. THEIR PATH LEADS THEM TO THE EASTERN BORDER OF THE KINGDOM.

HERE THEY MEET A DELEGATION FROM THE INNER LANDS.
"GREETINGS FROM HALP ATLA, KING OF THE INNER LANDS, TO AGUAR, KING OF THULE! HE ASKS YOUR HELP IN SAVING HIS KINGDOM FROM THE GIANT KARAK, WHOSE POWER STRIKES TERROR IN THE HEARTS OF ALL WHO OPPOSE HIM."
"WELL, SIRE," SAYS VAL, "IT LOOKS AS IF VACATION IS OVER. BACK TO WORK."

NEXT WEEK— **The Giant Karak**

1960   © King Features Syndicate, Inc., 1974. World rights reserved.   9-1

1960

Prince Valiant
IN THE DAYS OF KING ARTHUR
BY HAL FOSTER

Our Story: HALP ATLA, KING OF THE INNER LANDS, APPEALS TO HIS NEIGHBOR, KING AGUAR OF THULE, FOR AID AGAINST THE GIANT KARAK AND HIS SAVAGE HORDE.

AGUAR AGREES TO SEND AID AND TURNS HOMEWARD TO RAISE AN ARMY. "I THINK IT BEST I RIDE TO THE INNER LANDS AND LEARN MORE ABOUT THIS KARAK AND JUST HOW STRONG HE IS," SAYS VAL.

HALP ATLA WELCOMES HIM WARMLY AND IS OVERJOYED THAT HELP WILL COME FROM THULE. THERE IS NO MUSIC OR LAUGHTER IN THE COURT. FEAR HAS CAST A SPELL OVER ALL.

"IT WILL TAKE MORE THAN SWORDS AND SPEARS TO OVERTHROW KARAK! HE IS HUGE BEYOND BELIEF. NEITHER SHIELD NOR HELMET NOR CASTLE GATE CAN WITHSTAND HIS AWFUL AXE. HE AND HIS FOLLOWERS REACHED THE BORDERS OF OUR KINGDOM A MONTH AGO. WE AWAIT THEIR ATTACK."

VAL DOES HIS OWN SCOUTING. HE FINDS THE NORTHERN BORDER MARKED BY A BRAWLING MOUNTAIN STREAM BEYOND WHICH KARAK IS ENCAMPED. BUT WHY DOES HE HESITATE? SURELY THE STREAM CAN BE BRIDGED OR EVEN FORDED.

AS HE TURNS TO LEAVE, A SCARECROW FIGURE RISES FROM THE WEEDS AND CRIES FOR MERCY.

© King Features Syndicate, Inc., 1974. World rights reserved.

"I WAS KARAK'S SKALD, BUT HE DID NOT LIKE MY MUSIC AND HAD ME THROWN INTO THE RIVER. HE FEARS THE WATER AND THINKS DROWNING THE MOST HORRIBLE DEATH. I HID BENEATH AN OVERHANGING ROCK."

"TOO LATE I FOUND HE LIKED NURSERY SONGS AND CHILDREN'S TUNES." VAL IS LOST IN THOUGHT FOR A MOMENT.... "GIVE ME YOUR LUTE," HE SAYS. "KARAK IS GOING TO HAVE A NEW SKALD."

1961

NEXT WEEK- The Bridge

9-8

Prince Valiant IN THE DAYS OF KING ARTHUR
BY HAL FOSTER

Our Story: PRINCE VALIANT TAKES UP THE OLD SINGER'S LUTE. "I WILL BECOME KARAK'S SKALD AND LEARN THE SECRET OF HIS POWERS."

"NO! NO! DON'T GO NEAR THAT MAD MONSTER. BETTER TO STAY THIS SIDE OF THE RIVER, FOR KARAK HAS A GREAT FEAR OF WATER AND WILL NOT CROSS UNTIL A BRIDGE IS BUILT."

THEY FOLLOW THE BRAWLING STREAM WHILE THE OLD MINSTREL TELLS OF THE HORROR EXPERIENCED IN KARAK'S MEADHALL.

WHERE THE RIVER WIDENS AND FLOWS GENTLY OVER A GRAVEL BED, A BRIDGE IS UNDER CONSTRUCTION. UNTIL IT IS FINISHED, THE INNER LANDS WILL BE SAFE FROM INVASION.

NIGHT FALLS, THE WORKERS LEAVE, AND VAL ENTERS THE RIVER. THE CROSSING IS EASY, BUT HE COULD NEVER HAVE MANAGED IT ENCUMBERED WITH SHIELD AND ARMOR.

THE OLD TROUBADOUR LIMPS INTO HALP ATLA'S STRONGHOLD AND TELLS OF THE STRANGE BATTLE PLAN VAL HAS SUGGESTED.

VAL DOES NOT BELIEVE IN GIANTS, BUT AT SIGHT OF THE HUGE HALL, THE MASSIVE TIMBERS AND WIDE DOOR, HE HAS MISGIVINGS. FIERCE ARMED MEN RUSH OUT AND SURROUND HIM, BUT AT SIGHT OF HIS LUTE THEY HESITATE; FOR THE PERSON OF SKALD OR TROUBADOUR, STORYTELLER OR POET IS HELD SACRED AS THE ONLY SOURCE OF ENTERTAINMENT.

NEXT WEEK—*Karak, The Terrible*

9-15
1962

Our Story: PRINCE VALIANT WALKS BOLDLY THROUGH THE THREATENING WARRIORS, CONFIDENT THAT THEY WILL HONOR THE CODE THAT PROTECTS ALL SKALDS. HE IS ALLOWED TO PASS.

SINGING, HE ENTERS THE GREAT HALL AND HE, WHO HAS UNTIL NOW FEARED NO MAN, LEARNS WHAT TERROR IS.

KARAK IS HUGE. ARMS AND LEGS LIKE OAK TREES AND MIGHTY SHOULDERS THAT EXPRESS INHUMAN POWER. HE STOPS EATING AND LOOKS AT VAL WITH LITTLE EYES FULL OF MALICE, EYES THAT EXPRESS NO INTELLIGENCE WITH WHICH TO DIRECT THAT AWESOME POWER.

REMEMBERING THE ADVICE OF HIS PREDECESSOR, VAL STRUMS A NURSERY SONG AND THE MALEVOLENCE IN THOSE EYES IS REPLACED BY A DREAMY EXPRESSION.

NEXT WEEK— *Trouble at the Bridge* 9-22

1963

Prince Valiant
IN THE DAYS OF KING ARTHUR
BY HAL FOSTER

Our Story: AS LONG AS VAL SINGS NURSERY SONGS KARAK DREAMS QUIETLY, BUT WHEN HE STRIKES A FEW CHORDS OF A WAR CHANT HIS MAD EYES BECOME FULL OF MALICE.

QUICKLY VAL RESUMES THE SOOTHING NURSERY TUNES AND THE RAGE FADES. VAL GUESSES THAT THE LITTLE CRADLE SONGS BRING BACK MEMORIES OF CHILDHOOD DAYS WHEN KARAK HAD KNOWN LOVE. FINALLY, STUFFED WITH FOOD AND MEAD, HE SLEEPS FACE DOWN IN THE REMNANTS OF HIS MEAL.

VAL WIPES THE SWEAT FROM HIS BROW AND SITS DOWN. HE HAS DISCOVERED TWO WEAKNESSES IN KARAK: HIS ABJECT FEAR OF WATER AND HIS AWFUL RAGE THAT CAN BE CALMED ONLY BY MUSIC.

KING HALP ATLA IS PUZZLED BY THE BATTLE PLAN VAL HAS SENT HIM BY THE OLD SKALD. NEVERTHELESS HE SENDS HIS FORESTERS TO FILL THE RIVER WITH DRIFTWOOD, LOGS AND BRANCHES.

SWEPT DOWN BY THE CURRENT, THIS MASS PILES UP AGAINST THE BRIDGE PIERS, FORMING A DAM BEHIND WHICH THE RIVER RISES STEADILY.

A PANTING WARRIOR STAGGERS INTO THE GREAT HALL SHOUTING: *"THE BRIDGE IS DESTROYED, BUT NOT BY MEN. IT IS THE ANGER OF THE GODS!"*

KARAK LUMBERS TO HIS FEET AND TAKES UP THE GREAT SHIELD AND AXE HE CARRIES AT ALL TIMES. VAL FOLLOWS AT A SAFE DISTANCE AS THEY MAKE THEIR WAY TOWARD THE BRIDGE.

NEXT WEEK— *The Water Demon*

1964   9-29

Our Story: GROWLING WITH RAGE, KARAK LUMBERS UP THE PATH THAT LEADS TO THE BROKEN BRIDGE BY WHICH HE PLANNED TO LEAD HIS SAVAGES INTO THE INNER LANDS AND MORE PLUNDER.

AT FIRST THEY FOLLOW THE RIVER, BUT WHERE A TRIBUTARY STREAM CROSSES THE PATH, KARAK TURNS INLAND. SO GREAT IS HIS FEAR OF RUNNING WATER, HE MUST FIND A PLACE WHERE HE CAN CROSS DRY-SHOD.

"LOOK, MASTER, WE CAN CROSS HERE," CRIES VAL, "IT IS ONLY KNEE-DEEP." THERE IS A BOULDER IN MIDSTREAM AND VAL KNOWS THE CURRENT WILL GOUGE A HOLE AROUND THIS OBSTRUCTION.

DELIBERATELY HE STEPS INTO THE HOLE. A GREAT SPLASH, A TERRIFIED SCREAM, AND VAL GOES DOWN. "THE RIVER DEMON! HELP!"

PANTING, HE SCRAMBLES ASHORE, SEIZES A PIECE OF DRIFTWOOD AND BEATS THE WATER TO FOAM. "A CURSE ON THE RIVER DEMON!" HE CRIES. THEN TO HIMSELF: "I HOPE I AM NOT OVERACTING THE PART."

VAL SEES THE TERROR IN KARAK'S EYES AS HE WITNESSES THE POWER OF THE RIVER DEMON. NOW TO USE THIS WEAKNESS TO THE MONSTER'S DOWNFALL.

1965 © King Features Syndicate, Inc., 1974. World rights reserved. 10-6

HIGHER UP, THE STREAM DWINDLES, AND GREAT LOGS FORM A CROSSING. VAL GOES OVER ON HANDS AND KNEES TO KEEP ALIVE THE FEELING OF FEAR.

NEXT WEEK — Disaster!

Our Story: A GREAT MASS OF DRIFTWOOD FLOATED DOWN THE RIVER AND LODGED AGAINST THEIR BRIDGE UNTIL THE PIERS COLLAPSED UNDER ITS WEIGHT. BEHIND THIS DAM THE PENT-UP WATERS FIND ESCAPE AROUND THE UNFINISHED END AND SCOUR OUT AN EVER-DEEPENING CHANNEL IN THE GRAVEL.

PANTING WITH RAGE KARAK TURNS, GRIPPING HIS AXE AND LOOKING FOR SOMETHING OR SOMEONE ON WHICH TO VENT HIS ANGER. "HOLD!" CAUTIONS VAL, "I CAN BRIDGE THE TORRENT."

"IN THE CALM WATER BEHIND THE DAM WE CAN CONSTRUCT A SIMPLE WALKWAY, BUT WHERE THE TORRENT RUSHES THROUGH, A TOWER WILL SUPPORT A DRAWBRIDGE THAT CAN BE LOWERED ACROSS THE GAP AND SO DEFEAT THE WATER DEMON!"

ONCE AGAIN THE WORK STARTS, BUT ALL THE NEARBY TIMBER HAS BEEN CUT AND THE WORKERS HAVE TO HAUL THE LOGS AN EVER-INCREASING DISTANCE, AND TIME FLIES.....

.....TIME FLIES, TOO LONG HAVE THEY REMAINED HERE. THE HUNTERS MUST GO EVER-FARTHER AFIELD FOR THE DWINDLING SUPPLY OF GAME.

1966   10-13

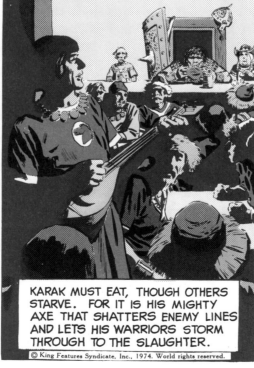

KARAK MUST EAT, THOUGH OTHERS STARVE. FOR IT IS HIS MIGHTY AXE THAT SHATTERS ENEMY LINES AND LETS HIS WARRIORS STORM THROUGH TO THE SLAUGHTER.

AT DAY'S END, WHEN FOOD AND DRINK HAVE PUT KARAK TO SLEEP, VAL SITS ON THE CLIFF ABOVE THE TURBULENT RIVER. THE QUESTION: WILL STARVATION HALT CONSTRUCTION OF THE BRIDGE?

NEXT WEEK - Lilies and Watercress

Our Story: EVER DEEPER INTO THE FOREST THE HUNTERS MUST GO TO FIND GAME; AND THERE, UNSEEN, THEY EAT MORE OF IT THAN THEY BRING TO CAMP.

THEIR SUPERSTITION KEEPS THEM AWAY FROM THE RIVER. BUT THE RIVER IS GOOD TO VAL. HE FINDS THE SPAWNING BEDS AND DINES ON THE SALMON HE SPEARS.

AT DAY'S END, VAL SINGS THE LITTLE NURSERY SONGS HE HAS COMPOSED DURING THE DAY; UNTIL, AT LAST, STUFFED WITH FOOD AND MEAD, KARAK SLEEPS.

THEN HIS MOTHER RISES AND DECLAIMS: "ALL HAIL TO MIGHTY KARAK, HIS IRON SHIELD NO SPEAR CAN PIERCE; NO MAN CAN BEAR THE WEIGHT OF HIS SHIRT OF MAIL; NO ARMOR OR CITY GATE WITHSTANDS HIS MIGHTY AXE! ALL HAIL!"

NOW THE PUNY LITTLE FATHER BECOMES FRIENDLY. IN HIS MOUSY WAY HE HAS GUIDED THE TRIBE, CHOSEN THE LANDS TO PILLAGE. LEADING THEM TO THIS RIVER WAS HIS FIRST MISTAKE, AND HE IS JEALOUS OF THIS TROUBADOUR WHO IS GAINING MORE INFLUENCE THAN HE.

"SON, THE BRIDGE IS NEAR FINISHED, WE WILL NOT NEED THIS VAL ANY LONGER. HE IS NOT ONE OF US, PERHAPS A SPY. TOMORROW YOU MAY CHOP HIM WITH YOUR AXE! HE-HE-HE!"

VAL CAN ESCAPE BY SWIMMING THE RIVER, BUT HE WOULD LIKE TO TAKE KARAK ALONG. HE DEVELOPS A SUDDEN FONDNESS FOR LILY BULBS AND WATERWEEDS, AND PICKS GREAT QUANTITIES.

© King Features Syndicate, Inc., 1974. World rights reserved. 1967

HE OFFERS SOME TO THE WARRIORS, BUT THEY REFUSE. MEANWHILE, THE SLIPPERY MASS ACCUMULATES ON THE EDGE OF THE CLIFF.

NEXT WEEK— The Death Sentence 10-20

1967

Prince Valiant
IN THE DAYS OF KING ARTHUR
BY HAL FOSTER

Our Story: KARAK RATHER LIKES PRINCE VALIANT, BUT HE LOVES KILLING EVEN MORE. SO HE AGREES TO FOLLOW HIS FATHER'S ADVICE AND SWING HIS TERRIBLE AXE.

"NO, NO!" LAUGHS THE MOTHER, "THROW HIM TO THE WATER DEMON. WHAT COULD BE MORE ENTERTAINING THAN TO SEE HIM STRUGGLING IN THE DEMON'S WHITE EMBRACE?"

VAL CAN SENSE THE ENMITY OF THE TRIBESMEN TOWARD HIM, A FOREIGNER. THEY FOLLOW HIM IN OMINOUS SILENCE.

THE STARVING WORKERS STRUGGLE CLUMSILY TO COMPLETE THE BRIDGE THAT WILL CARRY THEM ACROSS TO THE INNER LANDS WHERE FOOD AND PLUNDER IS PLENTIFUL. HE ESTIMATES IT WILL TAKE A WEEK OR MORE.

AT DAY'S END VAL ENTERTAINS IN THE GREAT HALL. NO FOOD IS SERVED. EACH MAN MUST FORAGE FOR HIMSELF; BERRIES, NUTS, ROOTS, MUSHROOMS. SULLEN EYES ARE FASTENED ON HIM...... AS IF EXPECTING AMUSEMENT OF ANOTHER SORT.

HE JUST HAS TIME TO GATHER THE SLIMY WATERWEEDS HE PRETENDS TO FEED ON, WHEN HE HEARS A MURMUR OF MANY VOICES.

TURNING, HE SEES THE PONDEROUS HULK OF KARAK LUMBERING TOWARD HIM, ARMED WITH THE GREAT IRON SHIELD AND AXE WHICH HE CARRIES AT ALL TIMES. VAL CRIES OUT IN FEAR AND MOVES BACK DANGEROUSLY NEAR THE EDGE OF THE CLIFF.

NEXT WEEK- The Demon's Fangs

1968

10-27

Prince Valiant
IN THE DAYS OF KING ARTHUR
BY HAL FOSTER

Our Story: KARAK ADVANCES, LAUGHING HORRIBLY, FORCING VAL TO RETREAT UNTIL HE HANGS OVER THE EDGE OF THE PRECIPICE.

WITH TAUNTS AND JEERS HE TRIES TO COAX THE MONSTER ONTO THE SLIPPERY PLACE HE HAS PREPARED, BUT KARAK RAISES HIS AXE AND THE WHITE CHIPS FLY.......IT IS NOW OR NEVER.

WITH A MIGHTY LUNGE, VAL SWINGS THE CAREFULLY PREPARED LOG. KARAK SCREAMS! SINCE CHILDHOOD HE HAS FEARED THE FABLED WATER DEMON. THE COOL WHITE ARMS OF THE RIVER ENFOLD HIM, AND THE SCREAMING ENDS.
NEXT WEEK–The Returning Hero

11-3

Our Story: KARAK DISAPPEARS FOREVER, WEIGHED DOWN BY THE HEAVY ARMOR THAT HAD MADE HIM INVINCIBLE IN BATTLE. VAL STRUGGLES TO THE BASE OF THE CLIFF AND FINDS A HANDHOLD.

THE TRIBESMEN LOOK ON IN HORROR AS THE FEARED 'WATER DEMON' CLAIMS THEIR LEADER.

AFTER A LONG STRUGGLE IN THE DARKNESS, VAL, BRUISED AND WEARY, CROSSES THE TURBULENT RIVER AND SETS FOOT ON THE INNER LANDS.

ON THE FIELD BEFORE THE STRONGHOLD OF KING HALP ATLA, THE ARMY OF THE INNER LANDS IS ENCAMPED AWAITING THE EXPECTED INVASION OF KARAK AND HIS MERCILESS HORDE.

KING HALP ATLA RUSHES FORWARD: "WELCOME BACK, PRINCE VALIANT. WHEN MAY WE EXPECT THE INVASION OF KARAK AND HIS SAVAGE MEN?"
"IN ABOUT A WEEK," ANSWERS VAL NONCHALANTLY. "I SHOWED THEM HOW TO BRIDGE THE RIVER."

"BUT KARAK WILL NOT LEAD THEM. HE WAS A NUISANCE, SO I FED HIM TO THE 'WATER DEMON.'"
"FATHER," SAYS ARN SHARPLY, "YOU ARE POSING LIKE AN ACTOR AWAITING APPLAUSE!"

"I HAVE BROUGHT AN ARMY ACROSS THE BITTER MOUNTAINS FROM THULE TO DO BATTLE. THEY HAVE SHARPENED THEIR WEAPONS AND THIRST FOR ACTION."

"AND THEY WILL HAVE IT!" CRIES VAL. "AT DAWN YOU MAY LEAD THEM TO THE BRIDGE ACROSS THE BOUNDARY RIVER AND HAVE FUN."

NEXT WEEK— **Child's Play**

1970 © King Features Syndicate, Inc., 1974. World rights reserved. 11-10

1970

WHEN ARN ARRIVES AT THE BOUNDARY RIVER, THE STARVING SAVAGES HAVE COMPLETED THE BRIDGE THAT WILL TAKE THEM ACROSS TO THE INNER LANDS WHERE FOOD AND PLUNDER AWAIT THEM.

AT SUNSET, THEY LOWER THE FRAMEWORK OF THE DRAWBRIDGE. TOMORROW, THEY WILL PUT ON THE FLOORING. ARN KINDLY PUTS IT ON FOR THEM.

THIS IS TO BE THE DAY THEY CROSS THE BRIDGE (THAT PRINCE VALIANT HAD DESIGNED), AND AT LAST THE LONG WEEKS OF HUNGER WILL BE AT AN END. THE WAY IS OPEN TO FOOD AND PLUNDER, BUT THE RISING SUN REFLECTS FROM A MYRIAD OF HELMETS AND SPEARPOINTS, AND HOPE VANISHES.

THEY GO INTO BATTLE WITH THEIR USUAL FEROCITY, BUT STARVATION HAS TAKEN ITS TOLL. THEIR RETREAT BECOMES A ROUT, AND IN PANIC THEY SCREAM FOR A MERCY THEY HAVE NEVER SHOWN.

SOME ESCAPE INTO THE DARK FOREST, OTHERS TAKE SHELTER IN THEIR GREAT MEAD HALL. FIRE-ARROWS SOON SMOKE THEM OUT BEFORE THE WAITING ARCHERS.

THEN ARN CALLS A HALT, AND ORDERS THE SURVIVORS BROUGHT BEFORE HIM.

11-17

1971

NEXT WEEK— A Birthday

Our Story: THE REMNANTS OF KARAK'S ONCE FEROCIOUS TRIBE ARE BROUGHT BEFORE PRINCE ARN-- STARVING, OVERWORKED AND CONQUERED BY AN ARMY LED BY A TEENAGE BOY-- THEIR SPIRIT FOREVER BROKEN. *"THERE IS NO GLORY IN SOILING OUR SWORDS ON SUCH AS YOU. GO!"*

"WE GIVE YOU TWELVE HOURS START, THEN OUR ARCHERS WILL BE FREE TO HUNT DOWN THE STRAGGLERS."

A BATTLE IS WON AND A VICTORY FEAST IS HELD, BUT PRINCE VALIANT IS NOT IN ATTENDANCE. HE HAS REMEMBERED THE BIRTHDAY OF GALAN, HIS YOUNGEST SON, AND IS RIDING POSTHASTE ACROSS THE PASS TO THULE.

HE PRESENTS GALAN WITH HIS FIRST HORSE. TO SOME IT MIGHT SEEM A PONY, BUT TO GALAN IT IS A WARHORSE.

OH, THE THRILL OF BEING 'THE MAN ON HORSEBACK' RIDING HIGH ABOVE THE ORDINARY FOLK! BUT THERE IS A PRICE TO PAY.

A WARRIOR'S FIRST CONCERN IS CARE OF HIS MOUNT AND GALAN IS GLAD HE CAN WORK STANDING, FOR SITTING IS GOING TO BE PAINFUL FOR QUITE SOME TIME.

1972 © King Features Syndicate, Inc., 1974. World rights reserved. 11-24

THREE YEARS AGO VAL BEGAN TO CARVE THIS ROCKING HORSE FOR GALAN, BUT HIS TRAVELS KEPT HIM FROM FINISHING IT. NOW IT IS TOO LATE. HE WILL CARVE WINGS FOR IT AND MAKE IT A DECORATION.

NEXT WEEK- *The Improbable Journey*

Our Story: EVENING, AND ALETA ASSEMBLES HER CHILDREN FOR A HISTORY LESSON. THERE ARE NO HISTORY BOOKS, SO SHE RECOUNTS OLD LEGENDS OF KINGS AND HEROES AND HIGH-HEARTED ROMANCE.

IT IS TWILIGHT WHEN GALAN REACHES HIS ROOM AND THERE, SILHOUETTED AGAINST THE AFTERGLOW, STANDS THE WINGED-HORSE PEGASUS.

THIS IS THE HOUR OF DREAMING AND HIS FANCY TAKES FLIGHT. THE HORSE BECOMES BUCEPHALUS AND HE ALEXANDER. HE MOUNTS AND DRAWS HIS SWORD.

OVER MOUNTAIN AND DESERT HE GALLOPS, EVEN TO FAR INDIA, AND BEHOLDS FABULOUS CITIES WITH GILDED DOMES AND MARBLE TERRACES.

AND STARTLED PAYNIMS LOOK DOWN FROM HIGH BATTLEMENTS, THEIR JEWELS FLASHING AS HE GALLOPS BY, AND THEY WONDER IF THIS PORTENDS WAR.

ONCE A STRONG FORTRESS BARS HIS WAY AND HE CALLS FOR IT TO SURRENDER, BUT JUST AS THE GREAT BRONZE GATES ARE OPENING, DARKNESS FALLS......

......THE STARS COME OUT AND HIS TIRED IMAGINATION FALTERS. HE DISMOUNTS AND GOES TO BED.

AS HE BLOWS OUT THE CANDLE HE WONDERS WHAT TOMORROW WILL BRING. WILL HE BE JASON OR PERHAPS PERSEUS, OR MAYBE HE WILL RESCUE FAIR HELEN? NEXT WEEK—Maiden in Distress   12-1

1973

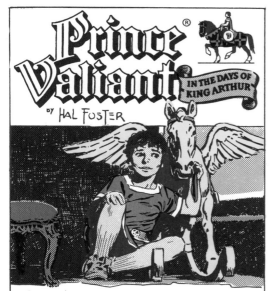

Prince Valiant IN THE DAYS OF KING ARTHUR by HAL FOSTER

Our Story: IN THAT HOUR WHEN THE SUN HAS SET BUT THE STARS HAVE NOT YET APPEARED, ONE'S FANCY ROAMS ABROAD. GALAN SITS BESIDE HIS WOODEN PEGASUS AND LETS HIS IMAGINATION TAKE FLIGHT.

AND THIS TIME HIS DREAMING TAKES HIM TO FAR ARABY WHERE ITS KING IS OFFERING HALF HIS KINGDOM TO THE HERO WHO CAN RESCUE HIS LOVELY DAUGHTER FROM THE CLUTCHES OF A GIANT.

WHO ELSE BUT GALAN? IN ALL THE OFT-TOLD LEGENDS THE HERO CUTS OFF THE GIANT'S HEAD, BUT THIS ONE IS TOO TALL. BRAVELY HE CIRCLES THE MONSTER, CUTTING HIM SHORTER BIT BY BIT......

.... UNTIL AT LAST HE LOPS OFF ITS HEAD, AND THE GOLDEN PRINCESS (ALL HEROINES ARE BLONDE) IS RESCUED! SHE FALLS IN LOVE WITH HIM IN THE BEST ROMANTIC TRADITION AND THIS ANNOYS GALAN. WHO WANTS GIRLS FUSSING AROUND?

SO GRATEFUL IS THE KING OF ARABY, THAT HE OFFERS THE HERO HIS DAUGHTER'S HAND IN MARRIAGE. NOW GALAN'S TWIN SISTERS, KAREN AND VALETA, HAVE TAUGHT HIM THAT GIRLS ARE, MORE OR LESS, MONSTERS. *"SIRE, I CANNOT FOR I AM A MARRIED MAN!"*

HIS DREAM WORLD VANISHES. *"I LIED, I TOOK THE COWARD'S WAY OUT!"* HE WHISPERS, *"MY HONOR IS TARNISHED!"*

1974

PEGASUS IS PUT AWAY, NO MORE TO CARRY HIS FANCY TO THE LANDS OF MYTH. A VERY UNHAPPY DREAMER GOES TO BED. A HERO WITH FEET OF CLAY.

IT HAS ONLY BEEN AN IMAGINARY ADVENTURE, SO IS IT NOT ONLY AN IMAGINARY LIE? HE WILL CONSULT HIS MOTHER IN THE MORNING.

NEXT WEEK-*The Fortunate Fracture* 12-8

Our Story: GALAN FOLLOWS HIS MOTHER ABOUT IN HER GARDEN. SILENT, SERIOUS, SO SHE KNOWS THAT HE IS TROUBLED. FINALLY SHE SITS. "COME, SON, AND TELL ME WHAT IT IS THAT WORRIES YOU."

"I LIED," HE QUAVERS. "IN IMAGINATION I RESCUED A DAMSEL IN DISTRESS, BUT THEN I REMEMBERED THAT THE HERO ALWAYS MARRIES THE PRINCESS, AND A LIE SPRANG READILY TO MY TONGUE. IS MY HONOR BESMIRCHED?"

ALETA LOOKS AT THE SERIOUS YOUNG FACE AND SUPPRESSES A SMILE. "NO ONE IS PERFECT, SON, WE ALL MAKE MISTAKES. JUST REMEMBER YOU ONCE LIED, AND YOU WILL BE MORE TOLERANT OF THE MISTAKES OF OTHERS."

HE BECOMES SO TOLERANT THAT WHEN THOSE IMPISH MONSTERS, HIS TWIN SISTERS, SET OUT TO TEASE HIM INTO A TEMPER, HE MERELY SMILES AND WALKS AWAY-- THEREBY SPOILING THEIR FAVORITE SPORT.

ANOTHER FAVORITE SPORT IS RUINED. VAL IS CARRIED HOME FROM A HUNT WITH A SWOLLEN ANKLE. WITH HIS FOOT IN A BUCKET OF ICE AND A SCOWL ON HIS FACE, HE WATCHES THE APPROACH OF GEOFFREY, THE COURT HISTORIAN.

"NOW, MY PRINCE, AS YOU HAVE NOTHING ELSE TO DO FOR THE NEXT FEW WEEKS, PERHAPS WE CAN FILL IN THE MANY BLANK SPOTS IN YOUR HISTORY THAT REMAIN UNTOLD." "TRIVIA," GRUMBLES VAL, "JUST TRIVIA."

GEOFFREY SETS UP HIS WRITING DESK AND PREPARES HIS QUILLS. "WHEN YOU WERE SQUIRE TO SIR GAWAIN, IT WAS HINTED THAT A LADY SAVED YOUR LIVES. WHAT IS THE STORY?" BY THIS TIME THE WHOLE FAMILY HAS GATHERED TO LISTEN, SO HE TELLS THIS TALE.

NEXT WEEK—The Story of the 'Lady of Quality'

1975

12-15

Prince Valiant

IN THE DAYS OF KING ARTHUR

BY HAL FOSTER

Our Story: AT THE REQUEST OF GEOFFREY, THE COURT HISTORIAN, VAL TELLS THE 'TALE OF THE LADY OF QUALITY.'
"WHEN FIRST I BECAME SQUIRE TO SIR GAWAIN, WE WERE ASSIGNED TO PROTECT THE LADY ALISON ON HER WEDDING JOURNEY.

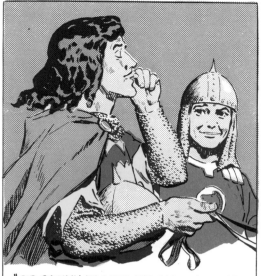

"SIR GAWAIN TOSSED HIS GLOSSY CURLS AND TWIRLED HIS MOUSTACHE: 'THEY TELL ME THE LADY ALISON IS THE MOST BEAUTIFUL WOMAN IN BRITAIN.'
"I GRINNED AND SAID THEY TELL ME HER FIANCÉ IS THE BIGGEST, ROUGHEST KNIGHT HEREABOUTS!

"THE BRIDE'S FATHER LIVED IN GREAT POMP AND SPLENDOR, AND EXPECTED AN ESCORT OF MANY FAMOUS KNIGHTS: 'TRY ME AGAINST TEN OF YOUR BEST KNIGHTS!' OFFERED GAWAIN. NO ONE ACCEPTED THE OFFER.

"THEN WE SAW THE LADY ALISON WALKING SLOWLY THROUGH HER SUNLIT GARDEN, LOVELY AS THE BLOSSOMS SHE TOUCHED. THE MOST BEAUTIFUL LADY IN THE KINGDOM!"

VAL STOPS HIS NARRATIVE AND LOOKS ANXIOUSLY AT ALETA. SHE IS POUTING.
"THAT WAS BEFORE I MET YOU, OF COURSE." SHE SMILES AND HE RENEWS THE STORY...

"OUR JOURNEY TO THE CASTLE OF THE BRIDEGROOM BEGAN WITH A BAGGAGE TRAIN AND NUMEROUS MEN-AT-ARMS. FOR THIS WAS EARLY IN KING ARTHUR'S REIGN AND VIOLENCE WAS THE ORDER OF THE DAY. THAT EVENING WE PITCHED HER PAVILION IN A BEAUTIFUL FOREST GLADE, BUT OUR LADY COMPLAINED:

'WHAT AN AWFUL WILDERNESS! THE ROADS UNPAVED, HEDGES UNTRIMMED, AND TREES ALLOWED TO GROW WILD. NOWHERE HAVE FLOWERS BEEN PLANTED.'"

1976 NEXT WEEK—Wild, Wild Flowers 12-22

Prince Valiant
IN THE DAYS OF KING ARTHUR
BY HAL FOSTER

Our Story: PRINCE VALIANT RESUMES HIS TALE OF 'THE LADY OF QUALITY': "IT WAS LATE WHEN WE BROKE CAMP, FOR LADY ALISON HAD TO CHOOSE HER GOWN FOR THE DAY AND BE PROPERLY CURLED AND PERFUMED.

"HER BEAUTY INSPIRED SIR GAWAIN TO HIS ROMANTIC BEST, BUT THERE WAS NO WORD OF FLATTERY SHE HAD NOT HEARD A THOUSAND TIMES.

"SIR GAWAIN RETIRED TO SULK AND THE LADY TURNED TO ME SAYING: 'WHAT A HORRIBLE WILDERNESS THIS IS, SHRUBS AND TREES LEFT UNTRIMMED, NO FLOWERS PLANTED.....!'

"THIS ANNOYED ME, FOR I LOVED THE NATURAL FORESTS. MY LADY, THERE ARE FLOWERS EVERYWHERE, NOT IN BEDS OR BORDERS; THEY DEFY THE GARDENER AND BLOOM IN THEIR CHOSEN PLACE. THERE IS BEAUTY EVERYWHERE FOR THOSE WHO CAN SEE BEAUTY.

" 'AND IS THAT PART OF THE BEAUTY YOU BABBLE ABOUT?' CRIED THE LADY, POINTING.
'DRAW!' BELLOWED GAWAIN, 'FORM A WEDGE, LADY ALISON IN THE CENTER! AT THE GALLOP, CHARGE!'

"WE CUT OUR WAY THROUGH, FOR THESE WERE OUTCAST MEN, UNARMED, SAVE FOR KNIVES, CLUBS AND STONES, BUT DESPERATION MADE THEM TERRIBLE. TO THEM DEATH WOULD BE A RELIEF.

"ON A DISTANT HILL A WATCHTOWER PROMISED SANCTUARY IF WE COULD REACH IT."
NEXT WEEK – The Siege
1977   12-29

Prince Valiant
IN THE DAYS OF KING ARTHUR
BY HAL FOSTER

Our Story: PRINCE VALIANT CONTINUES HIS STORY OF AN ADVENTURE WHEN HE FIRST BECAME SIR GAWAIN'S SQUIRE.

"WE LOST A FEW MEN-AT-ARMS BEFORE GAINING THE DUBIOUS SAFETY OF THE WATCHTOWER. SAFE, YES, BUT TRAPPED."

"THROUGH ALL THE TURMOIL THE LADY ALISON REMAINED CALM: 'THE CASTLE OF MY BETROTHED IS BUT FOUR MILES AWAY. PERHAPS A SIGNAL FIRE MAY CALL THEIR ATTENTION TO OUR PLIGHT.'"

"SO WE LIT THE FIRE AND THREW OUR WETTED CLOAKS ON IT TO CREATE A COLUMN OF SMOKE. NOW THE MOB OF OUTCASTS BROUGHT UP TREE TRUNKS WITH NOTCHES CUT FOR STEPS AND STORMED THE PARAPET."

"THEY WERE UTTERLY FEARLESS, FOR DEATH TO THEM WAS ONLY A RELIEF FROM THE MISERY IN WHICH THEY LIVED. GAWAIN DID NOT FORGET THE TRAINING OF HIS SQUIRE: 'DON'T JUST HACK,' HE ADVISED, 'THRUST, SLICE, CUT UPWARD, AND DON'T COVER YOUR EYES WITH YOUR SHIELD.'"

"THE ATTACK ON THE WALLS SLACKENED AND WE GLANCED DOWN..... THEY HAD BROUGHT UP A HUGE TREE TRUNK TO USE AS A BATTERING RAM, AND WE HAD NO ARCHERS TO HALT THEM! NOR WERE THERE ENOUGH MEN TO DEFEND BOTH GATE AND BATTLEMENT!

1978

"OUR ONLY HOPE WAS TO DASH OUT AND CUT OUR WAY THROUGH. SOME OF US MIGHT SURVIVE."

NEXT WEEK: The Lady of Quality

1-5

Prince Valiant IN THE DAYS OF KING ARTHUR
By HAL FOSTER

Our Story: PRINCE VALIANT CONTINUES HIS TALE: "BELOW US THE ENEMY HAD READIED THEIR BATTERING RAM. WE HAD TO SALLY OUT AND TAKE OUR CHANCE, FOR WE WERE TOO FEW TO DEFEND BOTH THE PARAPET AND THE GATE.

①

"THEN WE HEARD THE GATE OPEN AND CLOSE. 'BY THE GODS! TO THE RESCUE!' YELLED GAWAIN. BUT I SEIZED HIS ARM AND SAID, NO, WAIT, LOOK!"

②

"LADY ALISON, THE MOST BEAUTIFUL WOMAN IN ALL BRITAIN, RODE FORTH. HER PALE FACE WAS CALM, SHE LOOKED NEITHER TO RIGHT NOR LEFT. AS SHE WALKED HER MOUNT THROUGH THE MOB, THEY OPENED A WAY AND LOWERED THEIR WEAPONS. SAVAGES THOUGH THEY WERE, NO ONE WANTED TO BE THE FIRST TO DESTROY SUCH A THING OF BEAUTY. 'THERE GOES A LADY OF QUALITY,' SALUTED GAWAIN."

③
1979

NEXT WEEK: Finis   1-12

Our Story: "WITH MAGNIFICENT COURAGE THE LADY ALISON WALKED HER HORSE THROUGH THE RABBLE AND THEY MADE WAY FOR HER. THEY STOOD IN AWE, THEIR WEAPONS LOWERED.

"AT A SAFE DISTANCE SHE SET SPURS TO HER MOUNT AND GALLOPED TOWARD THE DISTANT CASTLE.

"WITH A HOWL OF RAGE THE OUTCASTS RETURNED TO THE ATTACK. BUT THEIR ARDOR HAD WANED, FOR WELL THEY KNEW THAT HELP FOR THE BELEAGUERED TOWER WOULD SOON BE ON THE WAY.

"IT WAS SUNSET WHEN HELP ARRIVED, BUT BY THAT TIME THE LAST OF THE OUTCASTS HAD MELTED AWAY INTO THE GLOOM OF THE FOREST. SO WE OPENED THE GATES AND RODE OUT TO MEET THEM.

"WE RETURNED TO THE CASTLE WITH THEM, OUR MISSION COMPLETED. LADY ALISON WAS DULY MARRIED TO HER BETROTHED. THERE WAS FEASTING AND DANCING AND ENOUGH LOVELY LADIES FOR SIR GAWAIN TO MAKE LOVE TO. A PLEASANT WEEK WENT BY.

"THEN ONE FAIR MAID MENTIONED MARRIAGE AND WITHIN THE HOUR GAWAIN WAS HEADING FOR CAMELOT!

"AND THAT," CONCLUDES VAL, "IS THE STORY OF THE 'LADY OF QUALITY.'"
"AND ARE YOU SURE YOU DID NOT FIND FAVOR IN THE EYES OF SOME OF THOSE LOVELY LADIES?" ASKS ALETA, SUSPICIOUSLY.
"OH, CERTAINLY," ANSWERS VAL TEASINGLY, "BUT I WAS VERY YOUNG IN THOSE DAYS SO IT WAS JUST THEIR MOTHERLY INSTINCTS."
"LECHER!" SNAPS ALETA.

NEXT WEEK— Back to Work   1-19

1980

Our Story: PRINCE VALIANT NURSES A TWISTED ANKLE AND AS THE LONG DAYS PASS HIS TEMPER BECOMES SHORTER. IT IS RUMORED THAT HE EVEN SNAPPED AT ALETA.

IT IS NOT RECORDED WHO WON THE ENSUING QUARREL, BUT VAL LOOKS RELIEVED WHEN A SERVANT BRINGS A SUMMONS FROM THE KING.

"BOLTAR HAS RETURNED WITH INFORMATION OF GRAVE IMPORTANCE, FOR THE KING HAS CALLED THE COUNCIL INTO SESSION."

BOLTAR HAS A FRIGHTENING TALE TO TELL: "OUT OF AFRICA CAME A FLEET OF SHIPS LIKE A PLAGUE OF LOCUSTS. THE NAVIES OF THE INLAND SEA WERE TAKEN BY SURPRISE AND MONTHS OF TERROR WOULD PASS BEFORE THEY COULD UNITE IN DEFENSE.

"HAVING A FASTER SHIP I FOLLOWED. WHEREVER THEY WENT ONLY DEATH AND ASHES REMAINED. I AM USED TO WAR, BUT NEVER HAVE I WITNESSED SUCH FIENDISH BRUTALITY AS THAT MYSTERIOUS FLEET LEFT BEHIND."

"WE CAPTURED A STRAGGLER AND PERSUADED ITS CAPTAIN TO NAME HIS LEADER. 'BELLA GROSSI,' HE SAID, BEFORE HE DIED." 1-26

BELLA GROSSI, WEALTHY, AMBITIOUS AND RUTHLESS. SINCE BOYHOOD HE HAD PLANNED TO CARVE OUT AN EMPIRE OF HIS OWN JUST LIKE ALEXANDER, CAESAR AND ATTILA HAD DONE BEFORE HIM. SUCCESS IS WITHIN HIS GRASP.
NEXT WEEK— The Terror

1981

Prince Valiant
IN THE DAYS OF KING ARTHUR
BY HAL FOSTER

Our Story: EVER SINCE BOYHOOD, BELLA GROSSI HAD DREAMED OF RULING AN EMPIRE. WITH THAT PURPOSE IN MIND HE AMASSED A GREAT FORTUNE AS A BANKER AND MERCHANT. HE HAD NO SCRUPLES TO HINDER HIS PROGRESS.

THREE YEARS AGO HE PUT HIS PLAN INTO ACTION. HE VISITED THE HAUNTS OF CORSAIRS AND PIRATES AND UNFOLDED HIS AMBITIOUS PLAN:
"THERE IS TO BE NO PIRACY FOR THREE YEARS. YOU BECOME PEACEFUL TRADERS ..... UNTIL 'THE DAY'"

"...... I WILL SUPPLY MONEY AND MERCHANDISE, BUT ON ONE CERTAIN HOUR YOU WILL TURN YOUR SHIPS TOWARD THE RENDEZVOUS AND ARRIVE THERE ON 'THE DAY.'"

"GIVE UP PIRACY FOR THREE YEARS? IT IS OUR PROFESSION, OUR WAY OF LIFE."
BELLA ANSWERS: "AFTER THREE YEARS OF PEACE THE NAVIES OF THE INLAND SEA WILL GROW LAX. WHY SHOULD THEY BE KEPT IN FIGHTING TRIM WHEN THERE IS NO FIGHTING? THE SEA WILL BE OURS."

THE THREE YEARS PASSED AND 'THE DAY' ARRIVED, AND FROM FAR AND WIDE THE SHIPS CAME. THE RIFFRAFF OF THE SEA EAGER TO RAVISH THE CITIES OF THE WORLD.

BOLTAR WAS HOMEWARD BOUND WHEN HE SAW THE VAST FLEET BEGIN ITS VOYAGE OF CONQUEST. HE CONTINUES HIS STORY TO THE COUNCIL......

...."THEY LAID WASTE THE COAST OF AFRICA THEN CROSSED OVER TO ROME, LEAVING NO LIVING THING BEHIND. WHEN THEY TURNED WESTWARD I KNEW THEIR AIM AND SET SAIL FOR HOME."

"THEN THEY COME THIS WAY," SAYS VAL. "OUR FASTEST SHIPS MUST REPORT THEIR EVERY MOVE AT SEA, HORSEMEN TO FOLLOW BY LAND."

NEXT WEEK- *Suspense*

1982   2-2

Prince Valiant

IN THE DAYS OF KING ARTHUR
BY HAL FOSTER

Our Story: TERROR SPREADS THROUGHOUT THE NORTHERN LANDS AS BELLA GROSSI'S DREAD FLEET ADVANCES, LEAVING BEHIND ASHES AND DEATH.

HORSEMEN REPORT THEIR MOVEMENTS FROM THE LAND.

AND THE KING OF THULE SENDS RELAYS OF HIS FASTEST SHIPS TO BRING NEWS OF BELLA'S PROGRESS, AND ALL THE REPORTS ARE DREADFUL.

BELLA MAKES BUT ONE MISTAKE: CROSSING OVER TO BRITAIN TO SACK WINCHESTER. HIS MEN MEET WITH KING ARTHUR'S MOUNTED KNIGHTS. IT IS A COSTLY LESSON AND THEY ARE GLAD TO RETURN TO THEIR SHIPS.

KING AGUAR, VAL AND BOLTAR KEEP IN CLOSE TOUCH WITH THE ADVANCING MENACE. AGUAR SPEAKS: "OUR VIKINGS ARE SCATTERED FAR AND WIDE, AND WILL NOT TURN HOMEWARD UNTIL AUTUMN. WE MUST SEEK HELP!"

VAL LEAPS TO HIS FEET: "BELLA GROSSI WILL FIND LITTLE PLUNDER AS HE MOVES EASTWARD WITH WINTER NOT FAR AWAY. IT SEEMS PLAIN TO ME THAT HE AIMS FOR THESSALRIGA IN THE BALTIC!"

THESSALRIGA, RICH AND POWERFUL, WITH TRADE ROUTES TO THE EAST, NORTH AND SOUTH. UNCONQUERED STILL, THOUGH MANY HAVE TRIED.

NEXT WEEK— *King of the Baltic*

1983   2-9

Prince Valiant
IN THE DAYS OF KING ARTHUR
BY HAL FOSTER

Our Story: PRINCE VALIANT SETS SAIL FOR THESSALRIGA TO SEEK THE AID OF KING LEOFRIC IN THE COMING CONFLICT WITH BELLA GROSSI'S PIRATE FLEET.

IT IS NO WONDER THESSALRIGA HAS TURNED BACK ALL INVADERS. HUGE TOWERS AT THE END OF EACH MOLE GUARD THE HARBOR.

AND ON THE LANDWARD SIDE, A FORTRESS PROTECTS THE WALLED CITY BEHIND.

VAL WASTES NO TIME IN TELLING LEOFRIC OF THE APPROACHING MENACE OF BELLA'S FLEET. TRUMPETS SOUND AND WITHIN MINUTES THE WAR-CAPTAINS GATHER.

AND WITHIN THE HOUR PREPARATIONS FOR WAR ARE UNDER WAY. LEOFRIC TURNS TO VAL: "BECAUSE OUR ISLAND IS SMALL AND OUR WEALTH GREAT, MANY A WAR LORD HAS TRIED TO CONQUER US. ALL HAVE FAILED."

BY DAY'S END THE DEFENSES ARE COMPLETE. THERE IS NO PLACE ON THIS ROCKY ISLAND WHERE A SHIP COULD LAND SAVE THE HARBOR, AND WHEN THE GREAT CHAIN ACROSS THE CHANNEL IS RAISED, THESSALRIGA IS SAFE.

A MAID OF NOBLE BEARING STOPS HIM. "SIR VALIANT, YOU HAVE WON FAME WITH SWORD AND SHIELD. WILL YOU INSTRUCT CROWN PRINCE ODO IN THE ART OF COMBAT?"

ONE GLANCE AT ODO AND IT IS PLAIN HE WILL NEVER BE A WARRIOR. THE MIGHTY KING OF THESSALRIGA HAS SPAWNED AN INCOMPETENT.

1984   NEXT WEEK – *The Ways of Odo*   2-16

Our Story: AT THE REQUEST OF PRINCESS GRANIA, PRINCE VALIANT TRIES TO INSTRUCT THE CROWN PRINCE ODO IN THE WARRIOR ARTS. ODO'S FEEBLE EFFORTS BRING A LOOK OF CONTEMPT INTO GRANIA'S EYES.

WITH AN ANGRY SNARL, ODO THROWS DOWN HIS BLADE. "I AM NO BEEFY WARRIOR! I AM A PHILOSOPHER, A SCIENTIST, A POET! WHEN MY TIME COMES I'LL RULE THESSALRIGA WITH BRAINS, NOT BRAWN!"

"YOU ARE A LITTLE SHY OF BOTH," MUTTERS VAL AS HE LEAVES THE ROOM. GRANIA IS STANDING IN THE HALL. TEARS OF SHAME GLISTEN ON HER CHEEKS. "SHE LOVES HIM! HOW CAN SUCH A PROUD BEAUTY LOVE A CLOD LIKE ODO?" VAL MUSES.

MORE IMPORTANT EVENTS ARE TAKING SHAPE. VAL'S SHIP RETURNS AND REPORTS: "WE COULD NOT RETURN TO THULE, FOR THE DREAD FLEET OF BELLA GROSSI FILLS THE STRAIT BETWEEN DANELAND AND THULE. THEY CAN ONLY BE A FEW DAYS BEHIND US."

AND YET ANOTHER SHIP ARRIVES BRINGING A GREAT PERSONAGE, EARL DUPUY, LORD HIGH CHANCELLOR TO KING LEOFRIC OF THESSALRIGA, NOW RETURNING TO REPORT ON HIS EFFORTS TO ENLIST THE HELP OF THE DANES.

IN THE THRONE ROOM HE GIVES HIS REPORT: "NO, THE DANES WILL NOT SEND HELP. IN FACT, THEY HOPE TO TURN BACK BELLA GROSSI AND HIS WHOLE FLEET." AND THE FLEET? "OH, WORKING ITS WAY NEARER, PLUNDERING AS IT GOES. IT MIGHT NEVER GET HERE!"

DUPUY IS SECOND IN COMMAND UNDER KING LEOFRIC, HIS LOYALTY BEYOND QUESTION. YET, HIS REPORT DIFFERS FROM THAT OF VAL'S SAILORS. PERHAPS THE SAILORS HAVE EXAGGERATED.

NEXT WEEK- The Inventor

1985   2-23

Prince Valiant IN THE DAYS OF KING ARTHUR

By HAL FOSTER

Our Story: IF PRINCE VALIANT HAS ANY DOUBTS OF DUPUY'S LOYALTY, THEY ARE SOON DISPELLED. WITH BOUNDLESS ENERGY HE ALMOST STRIPS THE FORTRESS OF ITS WAR MACHINES TO REINFORCE THE HARBOR DEFENSES.

HE SHOWS VAL THE GREAT MACHINE THAT RAISES THE CHAIN THAT SEALS THE HARBOR MOUTH. SO PERFECTLY COUNTERBALANCED THAT ONE MAN CAN OPERATE IT.

CROWN PRINCE ODO, BORED WITH ALL THESE WARLIKE PREPARATIONS, RIDES UP TO THE CITY AND DISMOUNTS IN HIS USUAL WAY BEFORE THE PALACE. THIS IS HIS FAVORITE HOUR.

NOW HIS WISE MEN GATHER AND READ THE WORKS OF POETS AND PHILOSOPHERS. AND IN A SONOROUS VOICE ODO QUOTES THESE LINES, FOR HE FANCIES HIMSELF A SAGE, THOUGH HE HARDLY UNDERSTANDS THEIR MEANINGS.

THE PRINCESS GRANIA LOOKS AT THE POSTURING CLOWN WITH SUPREME CONTEMPT. SHE HAS KNOWN HIM SINCE CHILDHOOD. PAMPERED, SPOILED AND INDULGED, WILL HIS MANHOOD EVER AWAKE?

JUST BEYOND THE HORIZON THE AWESOME FLEET OF BELLA GROSSI COMES FOAMING TOWARD ITS PREY: BEAUTIFUL THESSALRIGA, PEARL OF THE BALTIC.

WHILE FROM THE HIGHEST WATCH-TOWER, DUPUY ALSO WATCHES AS IF HE ANTICIPATED THE TIME OF THE PIRATES' ARRIVAL.

NEXT WEEK— *The Test*

3-2

Prince Valiant
IN THE DAYS OF KING ARTHUR
BY HAL FOSTER

Our Story: PRINCE VALIANT AWAKES TO THE BLARE OF TRUMPETS SOUNDING THE ALARM. THE ALL-CONQUERING PIRATE FLEET OF BELLA GROSSI HAS ARRIVED.

AS VAL CLATTERS THROUGH THE STREETS OF THESSALRIGA ON THE WAY TO THE HARBOR DEFENSES, HE IS JOINED BY KING LEOFRIC AND HIS SON ODO. AND ODO, AS USUAL, HAS GOT HIS REINS CROSSED.

THE ADVANCING FLEET IS AN AWESOME SIGHT. EVEN AT THIS DISTANCE THE DIN OF WAR DRUMS AND TRUMPETS CAN BE HEARD.

AT A SIGNAL FROM BELLA'S GREAT WARSHIP ALL SAILS ARE FURLED, OARS MANNED AND THE SHIPS MOVE FORWARD IN A LINE POINTED STRAIGHT TOWARD THE HARBOR MOUTH.

AS THEY DRAW NEARER; THE SOUND OF WAR CHANTS, THE BEATING OF SWORDS ON SHIELDS, AND THE WILD SCREAMING BECOMES DEAFENING. ENOUGH TO MAKE THE STOUTEST HEART QUAIL.

KING LEOFRIC IS NOT SHAKEN BY THE CLAMOR, FOR A PLEASANT SOUND HAS REACHED HIS EARS: THE SOUND OF THE GREAT CHAIN BEING RAISED TO SEAL THE HARBOR ENTRANCE.

DUPUY MAKES A FINAL INSPECTION OF THE DEFENSES, ENDING AT THE CHAIN TOWER.

1987 © King Features Syndicate, Inc., 1975. World rights reserved. 3-9

ALL THE CREW HAVE ARMED AND GONE TO THE BATTLEMENTS. ONLY THE CHIEF ENGINEER REMAINS TO ADJUST THE CAM THAT HOLDS THE CHAIN TAUT.

NEXT WEEK— 'Traitor'

Prince Valiant
IN THE DAYS OF KING ARTHUR
BY HAL FOSTER

Our Story: THE PIRATE FLEET COMES STRAIGHT TOWARD THE HARBOR ENTRANCE AMID A SHOWER OF MISSILES. THEY SEEM UNAWARE OF THE CHAIN THAT SEALS THE PASSAGE.

IN THE DIM CHAIN TOWER THE ENGINEER IS MAKING SURE EVERY DETAIL HAS BEEN CARRIED OUT. HE DOES NOT SEE THE SILENT FIGURE THAT ENTERS. NOR DOES HE SURVIVE THE AWFUL STROKE THAT FELLS HIM.

THE MURDERER RELEASES THE BRAKES AND THE CHAIN ROARS THROUGH THE PORT.... THE WAY IS OPEN TO THE CORSAIRS!
THEN HE TURNS AND HIS FACE IS REVEALED: DUPUY!
"TREASON!" HE SHOUTS. *"THE ENGINEER HAS RELEASED THE CHAIN!"*

NEXT WEEK – The Taste of Defeat

Our Story: "TREASON!" SCREAMS DUPUY. "THE TRAITOR ENGINEER HAS RELEASED THE CHAIN!" THE WARNING IS TOO LATE, ALREADY THE ENEMY SHIPS ARE ENTERING THE HARBOR.

TO RIGHT AND LEFT THEY TURN WHILE ARCHERS ON THE TOWERS CREATE HAVOC AMONG THE CREWS. STILL THEY COME, THE WHOLE GREAT FLEET, THEIR OARS BEATING THE WAVES TO FOAM.

DUPUY HAD STRIPPED THE FORTRESS OF WAR MACHINES TO MEET THE ATTACK FROM THE SEAWARD SIDE. THEY ARE SO CLOSE TOGETHER, THEY CANNOT BE TURNED TO MEET THE UNEXPECTED THREAT FROM WITHIN THE HARBOR.

SOON THE DEFENDERS IN THE TOWER WILL BE CUT OFF. "I FIGHT HERE TO THE END," SAYS KING LEOFRIC, "BUT THESSALRIGA MUST NEVER BE WITHOUT A KING. PRINCE VALIANT, TAKE CROWN PRINCE ODO TO THE SAFETY OF THE FORTRESS."

VAL DOES, BUT THEY HAVE TO FIGHT THEIR WAY THROUGH. "WHY DID YOU NOT USE YOUR SWORD?" ASKS VAL. ODO FROWNS, "I DID IT MY WAY."

1989   3-23

THE HARBOR IS NOW FILLED WITH BELLA GROSSI'S FLEET, BUT ALL THE FIGHTING IS AT THE CHAIN TOWER WHERE THE KING IS MAKING HIS STAND.

"BRAVERY IS FOR FOOLS," MUTTERS ODO. "MY FATHER IS A FOOL. BUT, AH, THE SPLENDOR OF HIS FOLLY!" HE TURNS AWAY TO HIDE THE TEAR IN HIS EYE.

NEXT WEEK- The Price of Peace

Prince Valiant

"HAL FOSTER"

Our Story: AT DAWN PRINCE VALIANT MOUNTS TO THE TOP OF THE FORTRESS AND SEES THE HARBOR FILLED WITH BELLA GROSSI'S SHIPS. THE CHAIN TOWERS WHERE THE KING AND DUPUY HAD FOUGHT ARE AFLAME.

BUT DAWN BRINGS A POUNDING ON A POSTERN GATE...... DUPUY HAS ESCAPED!

"KING LEOFRIC HAS FALLEN INTO THE MERCILESS HANDS OF BELLA GROSSI," DUPUY SAYS. "HE WILL BE SLOWLY TORTURED UNTIL THE CITY SURRENDERS.

"THE TERMS OF A PEACE TREATY ARE: THE CITY TO BE THROWN OPEN TO HIS MEN FOR THREE DAYS OF PLUNDERING. THE CITIZENS TO BE SPARED IF THEY OFFER NO RESISTANCE."

"AS COMMANDER OF THE ARMY I SHALL SEEK A TRUCE AND TRY TO SOFTEN BELLA'S DEMANDS."
VAL IS ENRAGED. "THE KING WOULD RATHER DIE UNDER TORTURE THAN SUBMIT HIS PEOPLE TO THE RAVAGES OF BELLA'S SAVAGE PIRATES! PRINCE ODO IS REGENT DURING THE KING'S ABSENCE-- WHAT SAYS HE?"

DUPUY TURNS TO ODO, SMILING, "YOUR HIGHNESS, AS REGENT IT IS YOUR RESPONSIBILITY TO SAVE YOUR FATHER'S LIFE."

DUPUY HAD PLANNED THE DEFENSE OF THESSALRIGA IN A MASTERFUL FASHION AND YET ALL HAD FAILED. VAL BECOMES DOUBTFUL OF HIS LOYALTY.

GRANIA APPROACHES, "PRINCE VALIANT, ODO NEEDS A FRIEND. OTHERWISE HE WILL DO EVERYTHING DUPUY TELLS HIM TO...... AND DUPUY IS A TRAITOR!"

NEXT WEEK- Siege 3-30

1990

Prince Valiant IN THE DAYS OF KING ARTHUR

by HAL FOSTER

Our Story: VICTORY COMES EASILY TO BELLA GROSSI, FOR HE HAS USED TREACHERY. NOW, WITH HIS FLEET SAFELY MOORED IN THE CAPTURED HARBOR, HE TURNS HIS ATTENTION TO THE FORTRESS THAT GUARDS THE CITY.

ON THE MEADOWS BEYOND THE WALLS HE SETS UP A CAMP FORTIFIED BY MOUND AND DITCH. IN THE FOREST BEYOND, THE BEAUTIFUL AGE-OLD TREES ARE FELLED TO MAKE WAR MACHINES.

BELLA HAS BEGUN THE MOST HORRIBLE TACTIC IN WARFARE: THE SIEGE, WITH ITS STARVATION, DISEASE AND DEATH. AS ADMINISTRATOR, DUPUY SHOULD IMPOSE STRICT RATIONING; INSTEAD HE SPENDS HIS TIME WITH ODO.

PRINCE VALIANT FEELS HIS ANGER RISING. IN THE ENEMY CAMP EVERY MAN IS AT WORK PREPARING FOR THE CONQUEST OF THE CITY, BUT IN THESSALRIGA NOTHING IS BEING DONE. IT SEEMS READY TO ACCEPT DEFEAT.

"ONE GOOD TROOP OF MOUNTED KNIGHTS COULD DRIVE THAT RIFFRAFF INTO THE SEA!" VAL SAYS. AN OFFICER ANSWERS, "WE HAVE A CAVALRY UNIT, BUT IT COULD NOT DRIVE A RABBIT OUT OF A CABBAGE PATCH!" 1991

IT TURNS OUT TO BE A CEREMONIAL TROOP – POLISHED, GLITTERING, AND USELESS.

HOWEVER, VALIANT ASKS FOR COMMAND, AND BEGINS THE LONG HARD TASK OF TURNING DANDIES INTO WARRIORS.

NEXT WEEK— *Dupuy's Bonus*

4-6